GUIDES

WORKING OUTDOORS

REAL LIFE GUIDES
Practical guides for practical people

In this series of career guides from Trotman, we look in detail at what it takes to train for, get into and be successful at a wide spectrum of practical careers. The *Real Life Guides* aim to inform and inspire young people and adults alike by providing comprehensive yet hard-hitting and often blunt information about what it takes to succeed in these careers.

Other titles in this series are:

trotman

Real
Life
GUIDES

WORKING OUTDOORS

Camilla Zajac
2nd edition

Real Life Guides: Working Outdoors

This second edition published in 2008 by Trotman
Publishing, a division of Crimson Publishing Ltd.,
Westminster House, Kew Road, Richmond, Surrey
TW9 2ND

© Trotman Publishing 2008

First edition by Margaret McAlpine, published in 2004 by
Trotman and Company Ltd

Author Camilla Zajac

British Library Cataloguing in Publication Data
A catalogue record for this book is available from the British
Library

ISBN 978 1 84455 156 9

Typeset by RefineCatch Ltd, Bungay, Suffolk

Printed and bound in Great Britain by Athenaeum Press,
Gateshead

Real Life

GUIDES

CONTENTS

About the author

Camilla Zajac developed her role as a freelance careers writer whilst working in communications in the statutory and voluntary sector. She wrote for a wide range of careers resources aimed at young people, students and adults. Five years ago Camilla set up her own copywriting business and since then has written for communications and resources in the careers, charities and business sectors. She lives and works in Nottingham.

Acknowledgements

The author wishes to thank the following organisations for their help and support:

- Lantra
- Natural England

Foreword

If you enjoy being outside perhaps you should consider a career in one of the land-based industries featured in this book. Land-based industries cover sectors such as agriculture, forestry, horticulture, specialist engineering, conservation and animal care, each containing a broad range of career opportunities.

A high percentage of land-based jobs involves hard physical work and will require you to use expensive equipment and handle livestock, so it is essential that you have the right training and knowledge.

City & Guilds NPTC have over 120 qualifications to help provide you with all the necessary skills you will require when working outdoors. You can do a work-based NVQ, complete a skills test or study at collage. Whatever level you are at and whatever style of learning suits you, City & Guilds have a qualification that will meet your needs and get you on your way.

City & Guilds is delighted to be part of the Trotman *Real Life Guides* series to help raise your awareness of these vocational qualifications. For more information about the courses City & Guilds offer check out www.cityandguilds. com and you could end up being a groundsman for your favourite football club.

Introduction

A huge choice of careers, a wide range of training opportunities and roles in all kinds of places – working outdoors has a lot to offer. While the land-based sector has well-established roots in sectors such as farming and forestry, it's also developing fast in other areas. The land-based sector is one of the most varied, with opportunities in everything from fisheries to fencing and from landscape design to horticulture.

More than 1.5 million people work in approximately 400,000 land-based businesses and organisations in the UK. Many areas of the sector are developing fast, with a strong demand for new entrants and a growing choice of qualifications. The land-based industries in the twenty-first century have a lot to offer ambitious people looking for interesting jobs with good prospects for promotion.

There's no doubt the sector has its challenges, but these are balanced by a range of career options. Even the more traditional parts of the sector, such as farming, are evolving quickly, with new opportunities, for example in organic farming. There are options to work in garden centres, engineering companies, golf courses and leisure complexes, at home and abroad.

DID YOU KNOW?

Golf courses are increasingly being recognised as important landscapes that, with the right kind of management, can support a wide range of wildlife. The UK has over 3,000 golf courses containing more than 150,000 hectares of land. Figures indicate that up to 40% of golf courses may need regular management, leaving 60% available for wildlife activity.

Working outdoors is not limited to the countryside. There are jobs in land-based industries in all parts of the UK – urban as well as rural. Just think about the acres of parks, gardens, sports grounds and golf courses in and around towns and cities. All of these need specialist attention to meet the leisure needs of the millions of urban dwellers in the UK.

Working outdoors offers a world of possibilities.

Now more than ever, people are looking at how to take better care of the natural world and its resources. Most land-based industries are focusing on sustainable development, which is all about meeting the needs of today's society without damaging the prospects for future generations. Whether it is farmlands, forests or beaches, taking care of natural habitats is creating a growing demand for committed professionals.

So what could a job in a land-based industry offer you? Would you like a specialist job where you use your practical skills in a hands-on way, or a technical job where you are trained to use the latest high-tech machinery? Perhaps you want the sort of experience that would open up the possibility of working abroad or could lead to management opportunities? Whatever plans you have for the future, you could be very surprised at the wide range of career opportunities on offer in land-based industries.

The land-based sector is made up of a number of large organisations and many smaller businesses, with people working alone as sole traders, in partnerships or employing a small number of people. The average land-based business has 2.5 employees. This means there are opportunities for enterprising people who want to be their own boss and set up their own business. The jobs covered in this book fall into two groups, as shown below.

Land management and protection covers work such as:
- Agricultural crops and livestock
- Aquaculture (fish farming)
- Fencing
- Land-based engineering
- Production horticulture (growing plants, trees and flowers commercially)
- Trees and timber
- Forest ranger.

Environmental industries covers work such as:
- Environmental conservation
- Fisheries management (looking after inland waterways for angling clubs; salmon and trout)
- Game and wildlife management
- Landscaping
- Landscape design
- Sports turf and golf green keeping
- Working on private property, heritage sights and botanical gardens
- Working on commercial grounds, public parks and green spaces.

The good news is that unlike some other sectors in which there are more people looking for jobs than there are vacancies, the land-based industry sector is actively looking to recruit hard-working, ambitious young people. A target was recently set to bring in 25,000 new recruits between

DID YOU KNOW?

The land-based sector offers opportunities for everyone. Whatever your age, experience or ambitions, there are qualifications and routes into learning to suit you. You can follow an academic or vocational route and study full time or part time, at college or in the workplace. To find out more, turn to Chapter 6, 'Training'.

2007 and 2010. This means high quality education and training schemes are available for the right people, leading to career pathways, job satisfaction and great prospects. In this book you'll find out more about these opportunities, including what the work involves, what training is needed and what prospects are on offer. You'll also find information about land-based jobs, the education and training routes leading to entry into such jobs, and promotion prospects once you are working.

If you are not sure how much you actually know about the land-based sector, try out the quiz on p.15 to test your knowledge. Find out what some of the jobs are really like with case studies of people working in the industry, in forestry, horticulture, conservation and other areas.

The *Real Life Guide to Working Outdoors* also includes information to help you find out more for yourself about specific jobs, with addresses and websites of professional organisations and training providers.

Land-based qualifications plus the right kind of experience can lead to jobs abroad.

1

LYNN BURROW

Case study 1

AREA RANGER,
PEAK DISTRICT NATIONAL PARK

Lynn Burrow is an Area Ranger in the Peak District National Park, the UK's oldest national park, created in 1951. The Peak District National Park is 555 square miles and covers parts of the counties of Derbyshire, Staffordshire, Yorkshire, Greater Manchester and Cheshire.

Lynn has worked at the national park for 15 years. She previously worked as a Market Researcher for a local newspaper but left to work voluntarily with the British Trust for Conservation Volunteers (BTCV) and joined the part-time ranger training course at the Peak District National Park. After completing the training course she became a volunteer ranger for the national park as well as working as a part-time warden for her local county council.

Lynn points out that it was the combination of her degree in European studies (majoring in geography) and her volunteering and part-time experience that gave her the start she needed. After a year she moved into a role at the Peak Park as a full-time Ranger. After completing a postgraduate

I enjoy getting people excited about conservation — and doing conservation work with people who might never have been to the countryside before.

diploma in Countryside Management four years ago, she became an Area Ranger working in the White Peak area of the park.

What Does Your Job Involve?
'My job is a combination of conservation and education.

'On the education side, I work with local communities, for example, going into schools to talk to children about the environment and the Peak Park. I also take groups of visitors out for guided walks.

'Conserving the national park is a key role for rangers. Much of the national park is nationally, and even internationally, important for its wildlife and habitats. We provide opportunities for visitors and local people to help look after key habitats, like woodlands, moorlands, limestone heath and grassland so that future generations will also be able to enjoy their beauty. At the moment the national park is working on a pond restoration project and I will be carrying out some of the work, together with conservation volunteers.

'Many people who visit the area enjoy walking along the footpath network that criss-crosses the Peak District. Part of my job is to ensure that these routes are easy to use – so we install gates and signs and repair eroded footpaths.

'I act as a point of contact between all the different people involved with the park – we provide a link between the visitors, farmers and residents that we come across on a daily basis in the field and the ecologists, archaeologists and planners who work at the national park offices.'

Where do you spend most of your day?
'This is very much an "on the move" kind of job. Whilst I spend some time in the office working on the planning and development of projects, I'm out and about on site and visiting people for around 80% of the time.'

What aspects of your job do you most enjoy?
'I really enjoy the hands-on activities in my job, even when it's muddy! I also enjoy getting people excited about conservation – and doing conservation work with people who might never have been to the countryside before.'

What skills do you need in your job?
'Communication skills are essential as I need to be able to talk to people from all walks of life – from school children to board members or politicians. I need to be able to work independently, but also be able to co-operate well as part of a team!

'You need a very broad range of knowledge about countryside issues as well. From practical skills like drystone walling, to academic knowledge of ecology or archaeology, to understanding about countryside or rights of way law. This is something you can develop with training and experience over the years.

'This job isn't for everyone. You're often outside in the rain, up to your knees in mud, so you need to be able to cope with the practical side!'

What are you most proud of in your career as a Ranger?
'One project that particularly stands out for me is the Pilsbury Castle project where we helped local people find out

about the history of their area. Five years later I met some of the school children who'd been involved with the project – they still remembered all about it. It was great to know I'd helped inspire local people about the history of the area.

'I also really enjoy taking families for animated guided walks. These are special walks where the visitor gradually becomes part of the walk itself, first meeting characters from the past, then reading poems or memories and eventually carrying out a task that helps to conserve the landscape.

'It's also the simple things that give me a lot of satisfaction – for example when I drive past a gate or a stile and think, "I helped repair that!"'

What would you say to someone thinking about working as a Ranger?
'This can be a very competitive area of work to get into. Many people apply for a small number of jobs so you have to be very determined.

'To start with, get work experience with your local council or national park, if you can. For example, the BTCV has groups across the country and in the Peak District we have our own conservation group, the Peak Park Countryside Volunteers. The Peak District also runs a Ranger training course.

'You'll also need a good qualification in a relevant subject like geography, ecology or countryside management. Then you just need to persevere in applying for jobs.'

To find out more turn to Chapter 3, 'What are the jobs?' and Chapter 6, 'Training'.

2

What's the story?

Whether it is bird flu, major floods or the growing popularity of organic produce, land-based industries are rarely out of the news these days. But from running a commercially successful farm to helping to conserve natural habitats, this is a varied sector with its own particular rewards and challenges.

You don't have to look very hard to see the important role that land-based industries play. From the food on your plate to the care and maintenance of your local sports ground – people working outdoors have helped to shape what's around us, even in towns and cities. It's an essential industry, but one that's not without its challenges. With issues like food scarcity, climate change and competition with food produced overseas, the land-based industry hasn't had it easy. Yet it continues to be a varied and vibrant industry made up of seven sectors, 230,000 businesses, over 1 million employees and over 400,000 volunteers.

Whilst there are many specialist organisations in the industry, the sector is mainly made up of small businesses, 94% of which employ fewer than five people. Working in a small business affected by changing markets is undoubtedly demanding. But changes like these also bring opportunities for new entrants. This sector is made up of some of the most labour-intensive job roles, for example in farming and horticulture. Along with an ageing workforce and growth in many areas, has come a greater demand for new entrants. In response to the 1,700 job roles needing to be filled, a target was recently set to recruit more than 25,000 people into the sector.

There's a lot going on in the land-based industries right now. Farmers' markets are on the increase in city centres. Home-grown and organic produce is more and more popular with people interested in the quality of the food they eat and the impact of the farming of fruit, vegetables and animals on the environment. In 2006, organic food and drink sales reached the £2 billion mark for the first time. It's also the first time that sales of free-range and organic eggs have exceeded sales of eggs from caged birds. In fact, organic food sales are increasing at a faster rate than any other area of the retail market (Soil Association).

It's also likely that agriculture will have a role in keeping us warm or getting us from 'A' to 'B' in the future. Concern about the environment is boosting the development of energy crops or 'biofuels', which are grown to provide energy for heat, electricity or transport. Energy crops include oilseed rape, palm and soya and bioethanol made from crops like wheat and sugar beet. Recently there has been a great deal of public debate about whether biofuels are genuinely environmentally friendly – and about the impact of producing energy crops on levels of food production. These kinds of issues show how the land-based industry is constantly developing, along with its many rewards and challenges.

DID YOU KNOW?

More than 70% of the UK's land is dedicated to agriculture.

Conservation and environmental management are more and more important because of a growing interest in protecting natural and historic landscapes for future generations.

Growing public concern about living in a 'greener' way is also boosting the rural tourist industry, with more and more people choosing to take holidays at home in the UK rather than flying abroad. Aside from holidays, the countryside is an important everyday source of escape and leisure for lots of people. Visits to the countryside or to open spaces in urban areas are already an important source of recreation for around 50% of the population. Also, 20% of adults in England are actively engaged with the natural environment as members of conservation and recreation organisations (Natural England).

Climate change is also likely to shape the future of land-based industries. More than half of English farmers taking part in a recent survey said they believe they are already affected by climate change and nearly 70% expect to be affected in the next ten years. Whilst climate change could increase the cost of farming, it could also create new markets and boost the demand for locally produced food (Farming Futures).

DID YOU KNOW?

There are 47 local Wildlife Trusts in the UK, the Isle of Man and Alderney. The Wildlife Trust is the largest UK voluntary organisation dedicated to conserving the UK's habitats and species. The Wildlife Trust manages 2,200 nature reserves covering more than 84,000 hectares. The Trust's volunteers carry out a huge range of tasks such as community gardening, species surveying and looking after nature reserves.

The government recognises the valuable resource it has in its land-based industries and has schemes to help support the land, farmers and other land-based businesses. Between 2000 and 2006 the Department for Environment, Food and Rural Affairs (DEFRA) supported the industry through the England Rural Development Programme (ERDP). Similar support packages are running in Northern Ireland, Scotland and Wales. The ERDP is worth £1.6 billion and so far support has included:

- Over 137,000 hectares of land approved for conversion to organic production methods under the Organic Farming Scheme.
- 4,500 hectares of energy crops planted under the Energy Crops Scheme with 8,600 more approved during 2006 for planting in 2007 and 2008. The Energy Crops Scheme helps farmers to grow energy crops to be used instead of fossil fuels and help to reduce greenhouse gas emissions.
- Over 3,000 Rural Enterprise Scheme projects approved, creating or protecting over 14,500 jobs, supporting over 1,200 diversification projects, funding nearly 550 village initiatives and supporting more than 3,500 new tourism enterprises.
- Over 156,000 training days supported through the Vocational Training Scheme, leading to the achievement of over 17,000 qualifications.

Just recently the government agency, Natural England, announced it would spend an additional £72 million on the natural environment in 2008, an extra £68 million for green farming schemes and an extra £4 million towards protecting and enhancing the marine environment, improving biodiversity and other areas.

Whilst plenty of challenges still lie ahead, there are definite signs that a more thoughtful approach to the rural environment is having a positive effect. That has to be good news for anyone considering work in a land-based industry.

The focus is firmly on land-based industries for the future – and that means a range of interesting career paths. Jobs and career opportunities in land-based industries may be on the increase, but are they right for you? That's a difficult question to answer, because the jobs themselves are so varied. The qualities needed for an engineer are different from those for a landscape designer, forester or gamekeeper. It's probably fair to say that the work is so wide-ranging that there is something for almost everybody.

To find out more about the wide range of work available in the land-based sector, turn to Chapter 3 'What are the jobs?'.

The vast range of careers in land-based industries is matched by the wide choice of education and training opportunities, including university degrees, HNDs, National Vocational Qualifications (NVQs) (Scottish Vocational Qualifications (SVQs) in Scotland) and apprenticeships. A rough guide to wages in land-based industries is as follows, although it is important to remember that pay rates may vary in different areas and with different employers.

DID YOU KNOW?

There are 18.5 million gardens in the UK and gardening is now the UK's favourite active leisure interest. In fact, more than £20 million is spent on plants and other gardening products every year and the horticultural industry is the largest employer in the UK.

DID YOU KNOW?

Apprenticeships are available in the land-based sector and offer a chance to gain high-level skills, qualifications and experience while earning a wage.

- A farm worker can earn around £18,500 a year.
- A forestry worker can earn around £16,000 a year.
- A fish farm employee can earn around £15,000 a year.
- A park ranger with experience can earn around £19,000 a year.
- Managers working in a land-based industry can expect to earn £30,000 and upwards.

To find out more about training and job opportunities turn to Chapter 6 'Training'. One aspect of a land-based career which is likely to appeal to the more adventurous is the opportunity for self-employment. It is an area where small businesses thrive and where determination and hard work really can lead to success.

QUIZ

How much do you know about land-based industries in the UK? Test your knowledge and then check your answers.

1. Plug plants are:

   A. A rare type of plant?
   B. A plant used to prevent flooding in gardens?
   C. Young plants grown in large quantities in nurseries?

2. Dry stone walling is:

   A. A form of interior decoration?
   B. An ancient way of building walls?
   C. A form of rural sport?

3. A Site of Special Scientific Interest (SSSI) is:

   A. A type of nature reserve?
   B. A protected natural area?
   C. An area under scientific investigation?

4. Farriery is:

   A. The shoeing of horses and similar animals?
   B. The care of horses?
   C. A type of farming method?

5. Greenwood trades are:

   A. Traditional woodland crafts?
   B. Types of jobs undertaken in a forest?
   C. Systems for processing wood?

6. The harvest from honeybees is used in which of the following:

    A. Manufacturing?
    B. Honey?
    C. Medical applications?

7. Which of the following is not grown on UK farms:

    A. Rice?
    B. Oats?
    C. Barley?

8. Tramlines are:

    A. A walkway for ramblers?
    B. Parallel lines made in fields of crops?
    C. The name for a type of farming tool?

9. Which fruit is grown commercially in the UK:

    A. Cherries?
    B. Kiwi fruit?
    C. Bananas?

10. Free range eggs are:

    A. Eggs imported from abroad?
    B. Eggs laid by hens that are allowed some freedom of movement?
    C. Eggs from hens that are intensively reared in special cages?

ANSWERS

1. C. Plug plants are young plants, usually seedlings that are grown in large quantities in single cells of compost by nurseries and wholesale plant suppliers. Plugs are a

way of planting or potting up seedlings whilst protecting their roots from disturbance as much as possible. They are ready to plant and are at the stage between a seed and a fully-grown plant.

2. B. Dry stone walling is an ancient way of creating walls in the rural landscape using only stone and no mortar or cement. Dry stone walls are common in areas such as National Parks and are usually made of sandstone, gritstone or limestone. They provide shelter for all kinds of wildlife and because of the way they are built, are very strong. Whilst many stone walls are two hundred years old and some are older, the craft of dry stone walling is becoming more popular again.

3. B. SSSIs are natural areas protected by English Nature, the Countryside Council for Wales and Scottish Natural Heritage because of the presence of important plants, animals or geological or other features. SSSIs are the best wildlife and geological sites in the country and cover a wide range of beautiful natural habitats. There are over 4,000 SSSIs in England, covering around 7% of the country's land area. SSSIs are important as they support plants and animals that would find it difficult to survive in the wider countryside. You can find out more and search for SSSIs near you by visiting www. english-nature.org.uk/special/sssi/search.cfm.

4. A. Farriery is the shoeing of horses and similar animals and a farrier is a skilled craftsperson who makes shoes for all types of horses' feet. Farriers are more and more involved with working with veterinary surgeons and equine hospitals to provide corrective shoeing and surgical farriery. A farrier is not a blacksmith, but needs training in blacksmithing in order to make the shoes correctly. Around 2,455 people are qualified to work in farriery in Great Britain, and around 100 apprentices are taken on every year to train with an approved training farrier.

5. A. Greenwood trades are traditional woodland crafts that include coppicing and charcoal production, making fencing materials and creating handmade furniture. Their name comes from their basic raw material, which is 'green' or freshly coppiced wood that has been cut rather than sawn. Chestnut and hazel are the most commonly worked kinds of wood. These ancient crafts developed quickly in the mid-eighteenth century and then decreased in popularity. Whilst the estimated greenwood trades workforce of today is only around 600 (compared to the 25,000–30,000 in the mid-nineteenth century) the craft is starting to thrive again.

6. A, B and C. The harvest from honeybees of honey, pollen, wax and propolis are used for all of these applications. Bees are an essential part of our food chain and without them, one-third of the food we eat would not be available. In the UK about 70 crops are dependent on, or benefit from, visits from bees. Bees pollinate the flowers of many plants which then become part of the feed of farm animals. The economic value of honeybees and bumblebees as pollinators of commercially grown insect pollinated crops in the UK has been estimated at more than £200 million per year.

7. A. The UK climate is not suitable for rice cultivation, which needs both warmth and moisture. It takes three to six months for a rice plant to reach maturity, and an average of 5,000 litres of water to produce each kilogram of rice. Rice is eaten by nearly half the entire world population, and many countries in Asia are completely dependent on rice as a staple food. The four major rice exporters are Thailand, Vietnam, India and the USA.

8. B. Tramlines are the straight parallel lines that run through the soil in fields. They are put in at the time of drilling the soil. They allow the farmer to drive through their field to fertilise and spray crops accurately without damaging the surrounding plants. Birds use tramlines to land in the crop before looking for food and animals use them as a route through fields.

9. A. Cherries make up 5% of the UK fruit market, with 90% of production based in south-east England.

10. B. For eggs to be classed as free range, hens must be kept in barns with a series of perches and feeders at different levels. They must also have constant daytime access to open runs which are mainly covered with plants and with room for a maximum of 2,500 birds per hectare.

Were you surprised by your score? There's no need to take it too seriously. If you surprised yourself by knowing more than you realised, however, it could be an indication of an interest in land-based careers. Keep reading.

3

What are the jobs?

With so much going on, the land-based industry offers many different job options. Working outdoors covers a vast range of opportunities, from the practical to the highly academic, for people of different ages and abilities. This industry employs more than 1 million people. If you are drawn to outdoor work, are serious about your career and are reliable and hard working, there is almost certainly an opportunity for you. Read on for a brief overview of the main job areas in the land-based sector.

LAND MANAGEMENT AND PRODUCTION JOBS

Agriculture

Think about working outdoors and this is probably the land-based industry that springs to mind. Agriculture is the production and management of food groups such as vegetables, cereals and root crops in settings as varied as hill farms in Wales to large mechanised arable farms in East Anglia. Main farm types include:

- Dairy
- Beef
- Sheep
- Pigs
- Poultry

- Vegetables
- Cereals
- Root crops
- Non-food crops such as crops for paper/materials such as flax or hemp, specialist oils such as lavender, pharmaceuticals and energy crops (biofuels).

Pharmaceutical crops are grown for sale to the pharmaceutical industry with certain parts of the plant being used in the production of drugs. Energy crops are grown to replace fossil fuels, such as coal, in the production of energy such as electricity. Crops include willow, poplar, hemp, straw and miscanthus, a type of grass. Rather than concentrating on one crop, many farms are mixed – growing crops and keeping livestock.

There are good opportunities in the agricultural industry to specialise in an area of particular interest such as livestock management, responsibility for crops or the maintenance of agricultural machinery. Farmers in the industry are also responsible for managing the land in an environmentally friendly way. This involves protecting areas of special scientific interest, restoring hedgerows and experimenting with organic methods of growing crops.

There are approximately 23,000 agricultural crop businesses in the UK, employing

DID YOU KNOW?

Even though British farms provide the nation with 60% of its food supply, many people are unaware of the links between the food on their plates and farming. In a recent survey 4 in 10 people interviewed didn't know yoghurt is made using farm produce, 23% said they didn't know bread's main ingredients came from the farm and 22% of adults questioned didn't know that the meat for bacon and sausages comes from farms!

around 129,400 people. Of the total land surface in the UK, 74% is under agricultural production. There are also approximately 75,000 livestock farm businesses in the UK, employing around 304,200 people. Over the last 25 years, livestock production has increased by 22%, with the production of poultry more than doubling.

Aquaculture

Aquaculture is the breeding and rearing of shellfish and finfish (mainly salmon and trout) for food, and finfish for restocking lakes and rivers for angling. Fish farms keep stock in cages which are lowered into water. This way the growth of the fish can be monitored and there is no problem catching stock. The work includes:

- Maintenance of equipment and cages
- Making sure the fish are healthy
- Checking that rearing takes place in good conditions
- Keeping stock safe and protected from poachers.

There are more than 1,000 fish and shellfish farming businesses in the UK, on 1,500 sites and employing over 3,000 people. The main finfish species farmed are salmon (139,000 tonnes mainly in Scotland) and rainbow trout (16,000 tonnes).

Fencing

Fences provide an important function in all kinds of settings. They can be simple or high-tech, made of wire, wood, concrete or metal – purely functional or extremely decorative. The different types of fencing include:

- Motorway barriers
- Sports ground barriers
- Institution perimeter fencing
- Zoo and animal enclosures
- Agriculture, forestry and garden boundary fencing
- Security fencing to reduce vandalism
- Sound reduction fencing.

There are approximately 4,000 fencing businesses in the UK, employing around 25,000 people. The businesses range from large commercial companies to small self-employed contractors. The industry is made up of specialist fencing contractors and multi-skilled operators, for example, in the landscape and environmental industries, and the construction, local government, volunteer and forestry sectors.

DID YOU KNOW?

7 million visitors walk in the British countryside every weekend.

Land-based or Agricultural Engineering
This involves putting scientific, technical and engineering knowledge to use solving agricultural problems, and working with different types of agricultural machinery – from tractors to sprayers and harvesters. Job opportunities cover:

- Design and development work
- Testing machinery by using it on farms
- Working for a manufacturing company making machines selling machinery
- Carrying out repairs and servicing
- Contract work (carrying out work on farms, using high-tech machinery).

There are approximately 5,800 land-based engineering businesses in the UK, employing an estimated 23,000 people.

Forestry, Arboriculture and Timber Processing
What's the difference?

Forestry is the management of woodlands and forests, while arboriculture is the care and cultivation of trees and shrubs in areas such as car parks, gardens and grass verges. Together they make up the forestry sector of land-based industries.

Forestry work includes:
- Establishing conifer plantations for timber production
- Creating woodland of broad-leaved trees for game management
- Raising young trees in forest nurseries.

Arboriculture covers:
- Establishing new trees
- Carrying out tree surgery operations to make sure trees look good and stay healthy
- Designing landscaping schemes
- Carrying out contracts for tree care and tree planting.

Timber processing involves:
- Marking timber
- Measuring
- Sawing
- Transportation.

Within the trees and timber industry, it is estimated that there are over 10,000 businesses employing around

30,000 people. It is a popular area of employment, so there is competition for jobs.

Production Horticulture

Horticulture is the growing of vegetables, fruit, herbs and plants from small-scale to large-scale production for local, national and international markets. Businesses range in size from small private nurseries employing two or three people, to large production organisations employing hundreds of people in different locations. Retail selling operations include:

● Garden centres
● Nurseries
● Farm shops
● Pick-your-own centres.

DID YOU KNOW?

East Anglia is the largest horticultural producing region in the UK, followed by the East Midlands and particularly Lincolnshire and then the south-east of England, especially Kent.

As well as growing and selling the plants there are opportunities to work in research and technology areas such as:

● Hydroponics – growing plants without soil
● Automatic watering.

Many production horticulture businesses operate as farms growing vegetables, while others are based on extensive orchards. Some businesses are intensive and grow fruit, vegetables and mushrooms in controlled environmental conditions.

In the UK there are 9,646 production horticulture businesses employing 95,166 full- and part-time workers, as well as tens of thousands of seasonal or casual workers.

DID YOU KNOW?

City farms and community gardens offer green spaces and practical experience of working with farm animals and growing crops for volunteers and visitors in urban areas across the UK. City farms and community gardens now attract more than 3 million visitors and regular users every year – around 50,000 of these visitors are school pupils. There are more than 60 city farms, around 60 school farms, and about 1,000 community gardens in Britain. A further 200 city farms and community gardens are currently in development.

There are around 18.5 million gardens in the UK and gardening is more popular than ever. Gardening enthusiasts need support from those who develop, grow, sell and maintain plants. Production horticulture is a major UK industry and it is growing – offering a huge variety of opportunities. It is also one of the most advanced sectors within the UK, especially in the areas of research and development.

ENVIRONMENTAL INDUSTRIES

Environmental Conservation

Environmental conservation is all about using scientific knowledge to protect today's natural resources for tomorrow. This area of the land-based sector covers a wide range of activities, from recycling household waste to managing specific wildlife habitats. Jobs in this area focus on sustainability – working to make sure that decisions taken today consider the long-term well-being of the planet. This includes the protection of rural and urban landscapes, plants and animals, rivers, coastal zones and waterways. There are jobs at local level on projects such as recycling, and at national level, for example protecting areas of outstanding natural beauty, while international issues such as global warming are bringing countries together across the world.

There are estimated to be 4,900 organisations in the UK environmental conservation industry. A large number of the workforce is voluntary, casual or part-time, with an estimated 56,100 paid employees in total working in this sector alongside 200,000 volunteers. Jobs in environmental conservation are becoming increasingly popular, so there is growing competition. Gaining experience through voluntary work is one way of making yourself more appealing to employers. To find more about volunteering take a look at Chapter 8, 'Hands-on experience'.

Park and Countryside Rangers

These are the people who look after areas of countryside set aside for visitors such as country parks. Their work includes:

- Managing and maintaining the area
- Educating visitors – giving talks and keeping visitor centres up to date
- Protecting the area from vandals
- Taking responsibility for the safety of visitors.

DID YOU KNOW?

Our 14 national parks cover 8,862 sq miles, have more than 443 miles of coastline and are home to 433,000 people.

Fisheries Management

Angling is one of the most popular sports in the UK with sports and coarse, game and sea anglers spending around £3.3 billion every year. Jobs include:

- Conserving and enhancing freshwater fish and habitats
- Working for angling clubs and syndicates
- Employment in fishery trusts researching diseases that affect fish.

The fisheries management industry currently includes government-funded fisheries research, privately funded research (Fishery Trusts), commercial trout fisheries, District Salmon Boards, fishing guides and ghillies (someone who acts as a guide for hunting and fishing) and angling clubs. The Environment Agency is the largest single employer of people in freshwater fisheries work in Britain. Other employers include the privatised water companies, DEFRA and individual private commercial fisheries.

Game and Wildlife Management
This includes the management of wildlife habitats and populations such as deer, grouse and water birds. It can involve the breeding and rearing of game birds such as pheasant and partridge, which are then released into the wild, ready for the shooting season. It also includes wildfowling and coastal and estuary management of habitats for water birds. Aspects of the work include:

● Maintaining wild habitats, buildings and pens
● Checking on the health of the wildlife
● Protecting them from predators such as foxes
● Managing sporting estates and keeping them in good order
● Preparing and running shoots for guests and visitors.

There are 3,000 game and wildlife management businesses in the UK, employing 6,000 people, many with dual roles on farms and estates. This sector is also made up of at least 60,000 volunteers and occasional or seasonal workers.

Landscaping
This is the design, planning, creation and maintenance of designed landscapes, both rural and urban. These include sports turf, golf courses, parks, historic and domestic gardens and leisure facilities. It is estimated that the landscape industry is made up of nearly 8,000 businesses

employing approximately 140,000 people. These people are employed in a range of different sized organisations such as local authority departments, parks and gardens; domestic and commercial landscape companies; and small, self-owned landscape contracting businesses.

THE LIE OF THE LAND

Whilst it is impossible to predict exac ly what lies ahead for land-based industries, certain areas look likely to develop in the future, and with them, even more interesting career opportunities.

Growing concern about the environment could mean opportunities in environmental conservation increase in the future. Though entry may still remain competitive, there could be more career paths in areas such as the conservation of natural habitats and wildlife management.

It is also likely that UK-grown crops, both for energy and food, could become even more important in the future. The increasing interest in the quality of locally grown food could also mean an increase in opportunities in conventional and organic farms.

DID YOU KNOW?

Market research commissioned by Lantra, the land-based industries body, found that whilst most young people surveyed understood what is meant by animal care (77%), fencing (65%) and landscaping (57%), they were least familiar with the terms production horticulture (9%), farriery (13%) and equine (14%).

Land-based industries play a big role in many aspects of everyday life and the range of training and qualifications is developing all the time. So it's worth spending some time to find out more about the jobs that interest you and where they could take you in the future.

4

It's very
satisfying doing
a job where you
can actually see
the results of
all your hard
work. I find it
inspiring to
think that
people will be
able to see the
results of my
work in 40,
60 — even 80
years' time.

MATTHEW COPE

Case Study 2

OPERATIONS FORESTER, FORESTRY COMMISSION OF SCOTLAND

Matthew Cope is an Operations Forester for the Forestry Commission in Scotland. The Commission exists to protect and expand Scotland's forests and woodlands and increase their value to society and the environment. Scotland's forests are the most productive in the UK and make an important contribution to Scotland's economy through jobs in the wood processing industry, forest management, wood haulage and other industries.

Matthew works out of the office near Perth and covers areas of Tayside, Perthshire, Fife and Angus. The forest area Matthew covers is some 10,000 hectares.

What does your job involve?
'My work is focused on the operational side of forestry, making sure we manage timber production from the forests in the best way possible. So I'm responsible for planning, managing and supervising the harvesting of timber. I also oversee forest thinning operations and the restocking and establishment of the next generation of trees on previously harvested areas.

'I manage a wide range of forest types in Scotland – from pine plantations on sand dunes to oak woodland through to upland conifer plantations. We plant a diverse range of species including Sitka spruce, Scots pine, Douglas fir, European larch, oak, willow, birch, cherry and more.'

What happens in a typical day in your job?
'There's no such thing as a typical day! Every day is different but there are regular tasks I'm required to do. I spend about 45% of my time outside. When I am in the office I do things like discussing future work programmes, managing contracts, drawing up tender documents and creating area maps.

'When I'm outside I visit various sites, seeing contractors and overseeing our timber management activities, ensuring that high production standards are maintained while keeping to strict health and safety and environmental legislation and guidelines. We produce a wide range of products so harvesting operations need to be managed carefully.'

What kind of products does the Forestry Commission produce?
'We produce sustainable timber for all kinds of uses: saw logs to be made into sawn timber for use in manufacture or sale to the consumer, pallet wood, chipwood for chip board, pulpwood for cereal packets and paper, fencing material and materials for the biofuel market.

'It is my job to market the timber produced, either as standing forest for the customer to harvest themselves or by separate product once harvested and stacked at the roadside by ourselves.'

How did you get into forestry?
'I studied for my A levels and at that stage my family thought I would go into an academic role. There was even talk of a career in accountancy! However, when I discovered forestry I knew it was the industry for me. So I went on to do the forestry course at the University of Cumbria. I did an extra year to make the course up to a Degree and spent my sandwich year working for the Forestry Commission England, in Kielder Forest. It was a similar role to the one I'm doing now, but at a more observational level.

'After completing my course, I got a job as a Works Supervisor in the Scottish Lowlands. For the last three months I've been on a temporary promotion in my current job and am hoping it will become a permanent role!

'There are a wide range of routes into forestry with a good choice of qualifications and training. While I didn't do any volunteering in forestry, I wish I had done. Volunteering can be very helpful in gaining relevant practical experience. It can also stand you in good stead for job applications, as with all practical experience. I think the hands-on experience I gained in my sandwich year was a big part in me getting my first job after I completed my course.'

What Do You Enjoy Most About Your Job?
'Along with my temporary promotion, gaining the Institute of Chartered Foresters' Best Student award for my final year at Cumbria is the highlight of my career so far.

'It's great to be outdoors so much of the time, instead of being stuck in an office! It's very satisfying doing a job where you can actually see the results of all your hard work. I find it inspiring to think that people will be able to see the results of my work in 40, 60 – even 80 years' time.

'The poor weather conditions can make this job tough sometimes. Getting back out of the van after lunch in winter isn't always easy! But apart from those moments, there's not much I would change about my job.'

Any final tips for people thinking about a career in forestry?
'It's easy to get to know people in this industry as it's not a big sector. So get out and get to know people – be active in looking for opportunities. Don't forget to make the most of the professional organisations. The Institute of Chartered Foresters provides plenty of helpful meetings and seminars and has been very supportive throughout my career. It provides networking for students, opportunities for getting experience in forestry, a topical conference, a study tour and funding for technical courses or specific projects.

'Forestry is no longer all about timber production. Huge efforts and resources are put into recreation, community involvement, social development, conservation of species and habitats and many other diverse activities. So there are many different opportunities.

'As well as my role in the operational team, lots of other roles exist within the Commission such as wildlife rangers, recreation rangers, planning foresters, land agents, ecologists and many others.'

To find out more turn to Chapter 3, 'What are the jobs?' and Chapter 6, 'Training'.

QUIZ: IT'S ALL ABOUT YOU

Is working outdoors for you? Try our quick quiz and then find out more about the qualities you need to succeed in the next chapter.

Are you comfortable following a varied, but regular schedule of activities?

  A. Yes
  B. No
  C. Don't know

Do you enjoy working with your hands?

  A. Yes
  B. No
  C. Not sure

Do you like working as part of a team?

  A. Yes
  B. No
  C. Not sure

Are you comfortable spending periods of time on your own?

  A. Yes
  B. No
  C. Not sure

Do you enjoy spending time in natural surroundings?

  A. Yes
  B. No
  C. Don't know

Do you like animals?

- A. Yes
- B. No
- C. Not sure

Mostly As
A career working outdoors could be just right for you. Read on to find out about all the different jobs out there.

Mostly Bs
As you'll see in the featured case studies, working outdoors often involves spending long periods of time in the countryside or other natural settings. It can also be physically tiring. Take time to think about whether you would enjoy these aspects of the sector.

Mostly Cs
You need to think about the everyday activities associated with this sector – then work out if you can see yourself enjoying it. Read on for more about the jobs on offer.

5 What it takes

What did the quiz tell you about the qualities you need for working outdoors? While there are many different types of land-based jobs, suiting a wide range of personalities and interests, each one demands specific skills and personal qualities. Whether it's conserving the past, managing animals or producing organic food, working outdoors offers interesting careers in a range of locations. Not working in an office or commuting most of the time sounds great. But the reality of being outdoors every day can be tough and it's not for everyone.

ALL PART OF THE ROUTINE

Working outdoors often involves a wide and rewarding variety of activities. However, within this you may need to complete routine tasks on a regular basis. This could involve routine checks on plants or animals or a set cycle of maintenance work. Routine is an essential part of many industries, such as farming, horticulture and conservation so you'll need to be reliable and methodical. Are you comfortable working to a set schedule of activities or repeating some tasks several times a week, a month, or a year? With all this routine you'll need to be reliable, too. Many land-based jobs are in small businesses where there isn't room for anyone who comes in late, leaves as early as possible and takes frequent 'sickies'.

GETTING HANDS-ON

Repairing gates, visiting sites, checking the welfare of animals – practical work is an important part of working outdoors. While being outside can be pleasant in the summer, these jobs often require you to be out when it's rainy and cold – and with just a couple of layers of extra clothing to keep you reasonably warm and dry! You'll need a good level of stamina, physical fitness and manual dexterity (being good with your hands) to keep working hard in these conditions. It goes without saying that you should enjoy physical exercise and activity. Whether you're building fences or planting trees, it's very likely you'll feel tired at the end of the day, no matter how physically fit you are.

Most land-based outdoor jobs demand practical skills, although that doesn't mean that quick thinking and common sense aren't important as well. Many jobs require a practical approach to problems and a high level of manual dexterity. With so many jobs in the land-based industry involving activities such as bending, lifting and carrying, this sector may not be suitable for someone who has back problems.

> 'In this job you're often outside in the rain, up to your knees in mud!'
>
> Lynn Burrow, Area Park Ranger,
> Peak District National Park

BEHIND THE SCENES

Working outdoors isn't only about being practical. You may need additional skills for the behind the scenes aspects of the job. With so many small businesses in the land-based sector, you may need important additional skills in areas such as IT and financial management.

PART OF THE TEAM

Getting things done as part of a team is an important aspect of working in the land-based industries. Caring for the natural environment or managing practical resources, for

DID YOU KNOW?

Of the more than 60 million people living in the UK, around 1% work in agriculture. Between them these people produce around 67% of the food we eat.

example, usually requires the support of a whole team, so you should enjoy working with others. Small businesses can bring a great deal of job satisfaction because more often than not you are able to see the end results of your work, rather than working on one small part of a large project.

Many different people have a stake in the natural environment, such as farmers, local communities, schools, so it's also important to be comfortable meeting and working with different people.

WORKING ALONE

In balance with teamworking skills, you also need to be happy working independently as and when the job requires. This is more likely to be part of your job the longer your career develops. Working alone for short or longer periods means being able to manage your own workload and stay motivated. This could be when you're out on site or when you're back in the office planning your next day's work. You have a list of jobs to be done and it is up to you to make sure that when you finish work your tasks are completed. If the unexpected happens you need to be able to reorganise your time and prioritise your activities so that the most important tasks are done first and that you meet your deadlines.

(NOT) WORKING NINE TO FIVE

Jobs in this sector vary hugely and so do the hours you would work. However, many hands-on jobs in areas like farming and horticulture are well known for involving very early starts – from four or five in the morning. Others require you to keep working until a particular job is done.

You may also be required to join in with whatever activity needs to be completed so it is important that you are flexible in your attitude to your working tasks as well as your working hours. Certain times of year are busier than others and when problems arise, this can mean extra hours at work. This is true of any job, but because there are 230,000 small businesses in the environmental and land-based sector, such incidents are likely to happen more frequently. Especially as the average number employed per business is 2.5 people with 94% of these businesses employing fewer than five people. If it is important for you to work regular hours and to leave work on time, think carefully before seeking a job in the land-based sector.

CLOSE TO NATURE

Hills, parks, forests – do you enjoy spending time in natural settings? This can be one of the biggest rewards of working outdoors. You can get close to nature and actually have a hand in helping to preserve it in areas such as conservation. But working in natural surroundings can be hard

DID YOU KNOW?

Typically, it rains on about one day in three in England and more often in winter, though most years do see long dry spells. The Lake District and the western Highlands of Scotland are among the wettest areas of the country. The sunniest parts of the UK are along the south coast of England, where many places achieve annual average figures of around 1,750 hours of sunshine. The dullest parts of England are the mountainous areas, with less than 1,000 hours of sunshine a year.

work. You often have to stay out in the cold or wet until the job is done.

WORKING WITH ANIMALS

Whilst many land-based jobs don't involve working with animals – there is a good number that do. It's very likely you'll have an idea already about whether you're interested in working directly with animals. But it's important to consider that dealing with wild animals or large numbers of animals, for example, is very different to encountering them in everyday life! In many land-based roles there's no room for sentimentality – animals must be managed carefully and professionally. Think about the demands of protecting wildlife in a conservation role, managing animals in a gamekeeping job or caring for animals on a farm.

6

Training

With so many land-based jobs out there, it's not surprising that there are a wide range of ways to get into the sector. From academic routes to more vocational, hands-on training, there's a way in to suit you.

APPRENTICESHIPS

A popular way of entering a land-based industry is with an apprenticeship. These provide an opportunity to learn while working, and combine practical skills gained in the workplace with theoretical knowledge. The number of apprenticeships has risen considerably in recent years, from 75,800 in 1997 to over 240,000 today.

The new 'family' of apprenticeships is made up of:
- **Young Apprenticeships** available for young people aged 14–16 years, who are still at school. During years 10 and 11 (it is also available in year 9 in some schools) students spend a total of 50 days (on average two days a week) gaining practical experience in the workplace and the rest of the time in the classroom. Over this time you would work towards your final Young Apprenticeship qualifications, which are equivalent to 2–4 GCSEs.
- **Apprenticeships** leading to an NVQ Level 2, Key Skills qualifications and usually a relevant technical certificate too. There are no set entry requirements for Apprenticeships but they are generally aimed at people aged 16–24. You also need to be living in England and not taking part in full-time education.

- **Advanced Apprenticeships** leading to an NVQ Level 3 (equivalent to two A levels), Key Skills qualifications and usually a relevant technical certificate. These are also aimed at people aged 16–24, but there is no set age limit.

Similar training opportunities are available in Scotland, Wales and Northern Ireland. Details are available on the following websites:

- Scotland – www.careers-scotland.org.uk
- Wales – www.careerswales.com
- Northern Ireland – www.delni.gov.uk.

DID YOU KNOW?

There is no longer an age limit on apprenticeships. They are now open to all age groups.

Apprenticeships were once aimed at young people, but now there is no age limit. They are open-ended, which means that each apprentice completes the course in his or her own time. As a general rule, apprenticeships take around one to two years and Advanced Apprenticeships two to three years. Most but not all apprentices are employed and receive a wage from their employer.

Some employers ask for GCSEs in certain subjects and for particular grades, while others are more interested in the person, their interests and their enthusiasm for the work. People applying for apprenticeships may be asked to take a psychometric test, which is a written test giving the employer an idea of a candidate's personality and interests. Literacy and numeracy tests may also be given to measure a candidate's reading, writing and number skills.

Further information about apprenticeships can be found
by visiting your local Connexions office, or on the following
websites:

● www.connexions.gov.uk
● www.apprenticeships.org.uk.

DIPLOMA IN ENVIRONMENTAL AND LAND-BASED STUDIES

This is a programme of brand new qualifications aimed at
young people aged 14–19. It will be available in some
schools and colleges from September 2009 and across the
whole country by 2013. The Diploma covers areas such as
working with plants, working with animals, looking after
forests and wild areas and how to reduce our impact on the
environment. You can start to study for Diploma at age 14
(years 10–11) at Foundation or Higher levels and continue
right up to age of 19 at Advanced Level. The Diploma is
preparation for apprenticeships or other training or college
or university courses. It is made up of:

● **Foundation Diploma**
   600 guided learning hours
   Similar length of study to 4–5 GCSEs, grades D–G
● **Higher Diploma**
   800 guided learning hours
   Similar length of study to 5–6 GCSEs, grades A–C
● **Advanced Diploma**
   1,080 learning hours
   Similar length of study equivalent to 3.5 GCE A levels
   There is also a level 3 Advanced Diploma qualification
      as a subset of the Level 3 Diploma comparable to
      2 GCE A levels

- **Extended Diploma**
  This is likely to be a similar length of study as 4.5 GCE A levels

For more information visit the Diploma in Environmental and Land-based Studies website at: www.diplomaelbs.co.uk.

GCSEs

There is a wide choice of GCSEs, the main qualifications taken by 14- to 16-year-olds. Entry requirements vary widely between employers and the subjects needed for different areas vary, too. However, relevant subjects for land-based industries include: Maths, Science, Biology, Chemistry, Physics and Geography.

A LEVEL OR GCEs (GENERAL CERTIFICATE OF EDUCATION)

A level or GCE qualifications usually take two years to complete full-time at school or college but they can also be gained through part-time study. You usually need at least five GCSEs at grades A–C to study for A levels. You may also need to have GCSE grade C or above in English or Maths. Relevant subjects for land-based industries include: Geography, Biology, Chemistry and Business Studies.

NATIONAL VOCATIONAL QUALIFICATIONS (NVQS)

These are work-based qualifications gained while doing a job. They are a statement of how well an individual can perform a particular task, and of the knowledge and understanding he or she has in order to perform the job competently.

NVQs are available in England, Wales and Northern Ireland. Scotland has a similar range of qualifications known as

NATIONAL VOCATIONAL QUALIFICATIONS (NVQs)
SCOTTISH VOCATIONAL QUALIFICATIONS (SVQs)

WORK-BASED QUALIFICATIONS, OPEN TO PEOPLE OF ALL AGES, WHILE DOING A JOB

LEVEL 1

FOUNDATION SKILLS

LEVEL 2

OPERATIVE, SEMI-SKILLED TASKS

LEVEL 3

TECHNICIAN, CRAFT, SKILLED AND SUPERVISORY TASKS

LEVEL 4

TECHNICAL, JUNIOR MANAGEMENT SKILLS

LEVEL 5

SPECIALIST SKILLS LEADING TO CHARTERED PROFESSIONAL STATUS
AND SENIOR MANAGEMENT POSITIONS

Scottish Vocational Qualifications (SVQs). There are five levels of NVQ (SVQ):

- Level 1 covers foundation skills in an occupation
- Level 2 builds on these skills to cover the operative skills needed to perform semi-skilled tasks
- Level 3 covers skills at technician, craft, skilled and supervisory levels
- Level 4 covers technical and junior management skills
- Level 5 covers specialist skills leading to chartered or professional status and to senior management positions.

Individuals who have practical experience of doing a particular job can be given credit for the skills they already have, when working towards an NVQ.

BTEC NATIONAL QUALIFICATIONS
These are vocational qualifications leading to entry into either employment or higher education.

The Btec National Award
This is roughly equivalent to one A level or an equivalent qualification. It is graded at three levels: pass, merit or distinction (P, M, D).

The Btec National Certificate
This is roughly equivalent to two A levels or equivalent qualifications. The Certificate is double graded, for example, PP, MP, MM.

The Btec National Diploma
This is roughly equivalent to three A levels or equivalent qualifications and is triple-graded, for example, PPP, PPM.

BTEC courses are run in land-based subjects across the UK. Subjects vary from horticulture to fish management and from agriculture to land-based technology. For more information contact your local college or Connexions office.

DEGREE LEVEL

The days are gone when the only way to university then was sixth form and A levels. Today universities welcome mature students who bring with them valuable life and work experience.

Access Courses

Access to Higher Education (HE) courses provide a route into a degree course for people without the educational qualifications usually required for entry into HE. The courses provide supporting knowledge and skills needed for university study and lead to an Access to HE qualifications which is equivalent to Level 3 qualifications such as A levels. Increasing numbers of undergraduates enter university via Access courses. Information on Access courses can be found on the Access to HE website: www.accesstohe.ac.uk.

Foundation Degrees

These are degree-level qualifications that combine academic learning with work-based learning. Employers are involved in the way they are designed, and they aim to meet skill shortages at higher technician level. Foundation degrees are offered by universities working with

DID YOU KNOW?

There's a new resource to help people in the land-based industries build on their employability and develop their career. The Skills Passport is a formal record of achievement based on industry-approved job role standards which helps people in the sector keep track of their skills and qualifications. The scheme is run by Lantra and the Land-Force jobs website.

higher and further education colleges, which means courses are often available locally.

Flexible study methods such as distance learning, weekend and evening classes are specially designed to suit people in work, unemployed people and those wanting to work towards a career change.

A full-time Foundation degree course takes around two years to complete, and a part-time course lasts between three and four years. Foundation degree graduates often already have a job. They can go on to take a professional qualification or to study for an honours degree (which takes a further 12–15 months of full-time study, or longer if studied part time). There are no set entry requirements for a Foundation degree; offers of places are made by the university or college running the course. Often experience gained from work in a particular job is taken into consideration. Foundation degrees are run by universities and colleges in just about every area of the UK. The following is just a small sample of such courses:

- Agriculture
- Horticulture
- Arboriculture
- Landscape and garden design
- Landscape management.

BACHELOR OR FIRST DEGREES

Some colleges and universities run these courses on a part time or distance learning basis. When studied full time, a degree course usually lasts for three years, or four years in Scotland. Some courses offer students an opportunity to take a year out working in an approved job connected with the degree course. Although doing this means studies take longer, the benefits gained from such work experience can be enormous. They can result in a more impressive class of degree as students bring real-life experience to theoretical situations, and can be a great asset when looking for a job because employers look for hands-on experience as well as academic qualifications. Some universities and colleges ask for particular A level grades or equivalent qualifications, while others are more flexible, judging each application on its own merit and are prepared to consider experience as well as academic achievement. The Universities and Colleges Admissions Service (UCAS) website, www.ucas.com, provides a wealth of information about degree courses in the UK and the universities and colleges running them, together with entry requirements and weblinks to the colleges themselves. Today many degree courses combine theory with practical, hands-on experience. The choice of degrees is huge and includes:

- Agricultural technology
- Crop science
- Rural resource management
- Plant and soil science
- Landscape architecture
- Horticulture
- Sports turf science and management.

Master's or Second Degrees
Some undergraduates take a first degree in an academic subject that interests them, such as geography, history, politics, English or sociology, and then go on to study for a second degree or a diploma in a specialist area leading more directly to employment. This is an excellent way of enjoying study for its own sake, if the money is available.

The downside is that it adds significantly to the already high cost of a degree. Some Master's courses are run on a part-time basis or by distance learning, which makes it possible to have a job and study at the same time. Postgraduate diploma courses usually last for an academic year (September to June). Postgraduate degree courses include the writing of a dissertation, which is usually submitted the September after the course commenced.

Always consider this route carefully. Graduates going into land-based industries are in a good position to move into management level jobs, but this is by no means certain to happen. Gaining a degree is a costly business. It's essential to do your research thoroughly before applying for a place on a degree course. If you're not sure what you want to do, where or why you want to do it, there could be a lot to be said for gaining some practical experience before you make such a big commitment of time and money. Gaining some relevant voluntary experience can help you make an informed choice. As well as the wide range of qualifications, check the particular sector you're interested in for other opportunities. The National Trust, for example, runs its own three-year gardening training programme known as Careership, open to anyone over 16 years old. Other organisations offer placements that lead to qualifications.

Lantra
For up-to-date information on training and learning opportunities get in touch with Lantra, the sector skills council for land-based industries. On its website www.lantra.co.uk you will find information about careers, education and training including colleges and training providers across the UK.

access to

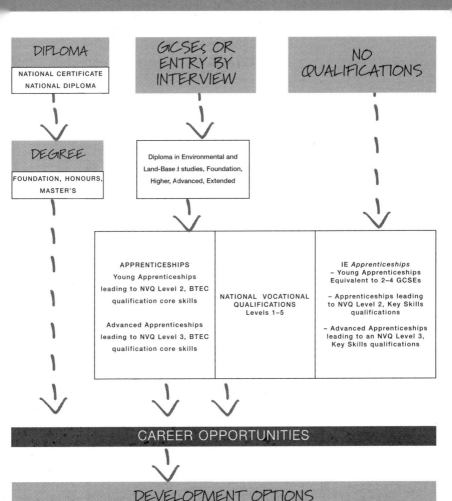

DIPLOMA

NATIONAL CERTIFICATE
NATIONAL DIPLOMA

GCSEs OR ENTRY BY INTERVIEW

NO QUALIFICATIONS

DEGREE

FOUNDATION, HONOURS,
MASTER'S

Diploma in Environmental and
Land-Based studies, Foundation,
Higher, Advanced, Extended

APPRENTICESHIPS

Young Apprenticeships
leading to NVQ Level 2, BTEC
qualification core skills

Advanced Apprenticeships
leading to NVQ Level 3, BTEC
qualification core skills

NATIONAL VOCATIONAL
QUALIFICATIONS
Levels 1–5

IE *Apprenticeships*
– Young Apprenticeships
Equivalent to 2–4 GCSEs

– Apprenticeships leading
to NVQ Level 2, Key Skills
qualifications

– Advanced Apprenticeships
leading to an NVQ Level 3,
Key Skills qualifications

CAREER OPPORTUNITIES

DEVELOPMENT OPTIONS

MANAGEMENT + SELF-EMPLOYMENT

7

DAVID TRICKER

Case study 3

PLANT AREA ASSISTANT, BURNCOOSE NURSERIES, CORNWALL

David Tricker works as a Plant Area Assistant at Burncoose Nurseries, the UK's largest specialist mail order supplier of garden plants. Burncoose specialises in plants such as camellias and rhododendrons, with many of the plants being raised and grown in the 30-acre woodland gardens at Burncoose and Caerhays Castle Gardens in Redruth, Cornwall.

David has been interested in working with plants ever since he was young and joined his father in helping out with conservation work at Kent High Weald, a designated area of Outstanding Natural Beauty. David also had a vegetable garden at home and enjoyed growing plants from seedlings. This interest has now developed into a career. David has a particular fascination for unusual plants and knows his *Metrosideros Excelsa* (a New Zealand evergreen shrub) from his *Knightia Excelsa* (New Zealand honeysuckle)!

What does your job involve?
'My job at the nursery is made up of a number of regular activities. I'm

responsible for weeding and watering the many plants the nursery grows and sells. We produce plants from seedlings so my job also involves seed sowing and potting up plants and moving plants from the polytunnels to the selling area when they're grown. I also serve customers on the till and help people with their enquiries. It's rewarding to help people identify a mystery plant they've found in their garden or to advise them on the problems they're having with a particular plant.'

What do you enjoy most about your job?
'Because of my interest in horticulture I really enjoy being able to give customers one-to-one help and advice about growing plants. It's also great to be involved with growing all kinds of unusual plants.

'I've just come back from helping with our display for the Chelsea Flower Show, one of the biggest events in the gardening year and a great opportunity to promote the nursery to thousands of visitors. I really enjoyed choosing plants and helping to build the display to represent Burncoose. It was also great to be able to pick up even more secrets behind growing and displaying plants!'

How did you get into your job?
'After completing my A levels in Biology and Geography I went on to do a degree in garden design at Falmouth, Cornwall. Cornwall is a great place to study horticulture because the milder climate means there's a wide range of plants. By the time I'd finished my degree I was more interested than ever in unusual plants!

'After my course I went on to do a year's placement as a Student Gardener at Tresco Abbey Gardens on the Isles of

Scilly. It's a fantastic site with 6,000 unusual plants. For a student relatively new to horticulture it was an amazing opportunity to get completely immersed in plants. My role at Tresco was to give guided tours of the gardens. The staff there really helped me think about what I wanted to do next in my career.'

What was your first paid job in horticulture?
'Because of my interest in growing unusual plants, I started on a trial period here at Burncoose as an Assistant Propagator. My job involved taking and growing cuttings of camellias and with 11,000 produced every season, it's a big job! That role lasted for six months. I've now moved on to working as a Plant Area Assistant.'

What are the most challenging aspects of your job?
'The wet and windy weather can be tough sometimes. Watering and weeding plants is a constant job and that can be hard work in any weather. But when the weather does get bad I can spend time in the polytunnels, where the cuttings are grown, taking care of the plants!'

Do you have any tips for people wanting to work in horticulture?
'Show a keen interest in plants – get to know the different types and how to grow them. Be willing to learn and show enthusiasm. You'll need to enjoy working as part of a team and be comfortable sharing your knowledge with others. There's a lot to learn in horticulture so don't be afraid to ask questions.

'Obviously you should be OK working in the cold and wet in winter! Try and get a placement somewhere that will give you great contacts and good practical experience. My own experience at Tresco Gardens on the Isles of Scilly has definitely held me in good stead for my career. I'm still applying a great deal of what I learned there. In fact I'm so enthusiastic about the experience my colleagues here call me "Tresco Tricker"!'

What's next for you in your job?
'After helping promote the nursery at the Chelsea Flower Show I'll be preparing plants and setting up for the next big show later in the summer – Hampton Court Flower Show. Longer-term I'm looking forward to building on my experience here at Burncoose and developing my knowledge of even more unusual plants!'

To find out more turn to Chapter 3, 'What are the jobs?' and Chapter 6, 'Training'.

8

Hands-on experience

There's no substitute for practical experience. Gaining first-hand knowledge of a job in the land-based sector will help you decide if a job working outdoors is for you. In a generally competitive job area like this, practical experience can be an invaluable way of making contacts and developing your career.

Many of the land-based professionals featured in this book mention volunteering or practical placements as an important way of gaining experience of a particular role. Some of them see practical experience – either as a long-term volunteer or through a one-off placement – as an essential part of their career development. Having practical experience on your CV will demonstrate commitment to a potential employer. See Chapter 13, 'Further information' for details of volunteer organisations.

THE FIRST STEP
Using this book and helpful information from the industry bodies, think about the specific areas in which you might like to gain practical experience.

Look at ways of fitting work experience into your life. Could you set aside a month or two of your summer holiday to gain some practical experience? Perhaps you could manage a regular slot every week.

Next, approach relevant local businesses in your area. Also take a look at what national organisations have on offer. They may have a volunteering scheme in place near you. Schools and colleges sometimes have volunteering schemes in partnership with local businesses. For smaller businesses you may need to get to know the company and send in a copy of your CV with an idea of the time you can commit to them. You may need to follow this up with a personal visit.

OPPORTUNITIES

Local groups

Look out for local groups that need the support of regular volunteers. Organisations such as the British Trust for Conservation Volunteers (BTCV), the Wildlife Trust and the National Trust have groups of volunteers throughout the country working on a wide range of projects. If you're looking for a one-off practical placement, BTCV and the National Trust also organise working holidays and weekend sessions. Visit their websites for details. You can also find out about placements in the land-based sector from Lantra.

> **DID YOU KNOW?**
>
> There are more than 400,000 volunteer workers in the UK's land-based industries. Around half of these work in environmental conservation.

Look around your local area. You might be surprised at the opportunities there are to gain practical experience of the sector. Even in urban settings there are possibilities for gaining vital hands-on experience, in city parks and gardens, for example.

Some national parks run their own training courses to develop the skills needed to work as a ranger or in countryside management. Contact your local national park for more information.

There are even opportunities to gain land-based experience abroad, particularly in areas such as conservation through organisations such as VSO and the Earthwatch Institute. The minimum age for VSO volunteers is 20. You will also need to have a good level of experience in your career. Whilst the standard minimum age for Earthwatch expeditions is 18, the organisation's Teen teams offer opportunities for young people aged 16 or 17.

9

LAUREN KINNERSLEY

Case study 4

VOLUNTEER

Lauren Kinnersley has worked regularly as a volunteer since 1991. She has been involved with a range of projects, mainly focused on conservation. Her interest in helping to protect the natural environment has taken her to places as varied as the Lake District and South Africa! Lauren balances voluntary work with paid employment.

What inspired you to become a volunteer?
'I felt concerned about what was happening to wild spaces and to nature. I wanted to contribute to a solution instead of focusing on all the doom and gloom.

'I started off by doing a one week "Natural Break" holiday with the British Trust for Conservation Volunteers (BTCV). I loved it so much I decided to become a full-time volunteer!'

What activities did you get involved with at first?
'I was involved with a project working on heathland in Dorset. The heathland is a rare habitat with species of snake and lizard found in few other places. The

It's very rewarding to get active and make a difference — and have a good time in the process!

heath was being encroached on by pine trees. The task involved felling the trees in order to preserve the fragile heath environment.

'It's very rewarding to get active and make a difference – and have a good time in the process!'

Have you ever worked full-time as a volunteer?
'Soon after my first conservation holiday I worked for six months as a full-time volunteer. Over this time I worked in Cumbria and the Lake District where our job focused on woodland management and access work – restoring areas to woodland and protecting fragile environments from heavy erosion by walkers.

'We worked on clearing paths, stiles and bridges. Our tasks also involved dry stone walling, laying hedges and planting trees. We were also involved with habitat management – clearing rhododendrons in woodlands, for example.

'During this time I was a group leader, responsible for taking groups of volunteers out for the day and coordinating their work and social activities! I was also responsible for giving a tools talk to the group to make sure they used the practical equipment safely.

'Leading groups of volunteers was a fantastic experience and a big responsibility. I needed to put my people skills as well as my conservation skills into practice!

'It was amazing to work in such beautiful surroundings. Another highlight was getting to work alongside other organisations like the National Trust. It was also a very sociable experience and great to meet people really trying to make a difference.'

Were you given any training for your role as group leader?
'I was given a range of training to help me prepare for leading the group, including leadership skills, working with tools and First Aid, as well as practical conservation skills.'

Have you done any other environmental conservation projects?
'I've also worked as a volunteer overseas! In 2003 I went to South Africa as a volunteer with BTCV. For three weeks, I worked as part of a group to clear a rare heathland site of non-native trees. This was to help protect the very rare flower that grows in abundance on the heath. It was great to stay with a family in the area and get to know the local community.'

What voluntary work do you currently do?
'I still volunteer in an outdoors setting, but in a slightly different kind of role. I'm now a regular Forest School volunteer in Nottingham one morning a week. At the Forest School I help run environmentally-related activity sessions in natural places, such as country parks and orchards, to help children build on their confidence, communication skills and general personal development. I spend time with the children guiding them through activities such as den building, working with tools and making objects out of natural materials.

'There's a lot of satisfaction in working with children on a one-to-one basis. It's great to feel I'm making a difference to their confidence. As well as supporting the kids' personal development, I'm also helping them to develop a positive relationship with the natural environment.'

10

FAQs

Asking the right questions is an important part of making a decision about any career. You'll need to do your own research to find the answers and decide whether working outdoors is still right for you. The best way to do this is by talking to as many people as possible working in the sector that interests you.

Carrying out your own research is very important. Working outdoors covers such a wide range of jobs that it is difficult to generalise about the industry as a whole. What is true for someone working on an organic farm may not apply at all to a person working as a gamekeeper or as a manager of a nursery.

HOW CAN I FIND OUT MORE ABOUT JOBS IN THE LAND-BASED SECTOR?

You will have learned more in this book about the many kinds of jobs available. The next step is to work out if you already know some jobs that might interest you. Take a look at the list of useful organisations at the back of this book. Many of them include further information about jobs on their website or provide useful careers information on request.

HOW CAN I FIND OUT WHAT A PARTICULAR JOB AREA IS ACTUALLY LIKE?

Great – you've found a specific area that interests you and contacted the relevant organisation for more information. After this, a great way to get the inside track on a job is to gain practical experience. A placement or holiday job will give you the chance to talk to people who are doing the job and help you think about whether the job is right for you. For more information on volunteering, see Chapter 8.

DOES WORKING OUTDOORS MEAN MOVING TO THE COUNTRYSIDE?

The land-based industry covers both urban and rural areas. Obviously, there are many jobs in the countryside but there are also opportunities to work – and gain voluntary experience – in towns and cities. Urban areas have green spaces and natural resources that need management too, like golf courses, greens, parks and gardens. There are also some opportunities in environmental conservation.

HOW LONG WILL I HAVE TO TRAIN?

How long you'll need to train will depend on your choice of job or sector. You can gain qualifications by taking full-time or part-time courses at a college or university. Work-based vocational training includes NVQs and SVQs and is available to people of all ages. Apprenticeships offer people an opportunity to gain qualifications while working in a job. In many cases the length of time taken to gain a qualification is flexible and depends on the individual. Gaining an NVQ Level 1 or Level 2 generally takes around one to two years. For more information on training for a land-based career, see Chapter 5 What it takes'.

WILL I WORK NINE TO FIVE?

In this industry, working days vary widely. Your working hours will depend on the type of job you are doing. You will be given time off, but in many job areas you will need to be flexible about the hours you work. In many jobs in this sector the work is seasonal, with employees working long hours at particular times such as harvest or during the summer fruit season. Flexibility is an essential part of many jobs, especially in small businesses. The land-based sector is mainly made up of companies that employ a small team of people. If you decide to follow the self-employment route and set up your own company you will need to be ready to work long and irregular hours.

WHAT KIND OF PAY CAN I EXPECT?
Again, in an industry this wide-ranging, pay rates vary widely according to job and location. A rough guide to wages in land-based industries is as follows: rates for farm workers are around £18,500 a year; a forestry worker earns around £16,000 a year; a fish farm employee earns around £15,000 a year; a park ranger with experience can earn around £19,000 a year. In some jobs, accommodation is an added benefit, or your uniforms or working clothes may be provided.

HOW MUCH HOLIDAY TIME WOULD I GET?
All employees are entitled to paid leave of 24 days every year. Many outdoor jobs are seasonal, with one part of the year being particularly busy. So employees are sometimes required to take their holiday at a certain time to make sure as many people as possible are on hand during busy periods.

IS IT EASY TO CHANGE CAREERS?
This depends on the career move you want to make. While some skills can be transferred between jobs, you would need to retrain for other career changes.

HOW IS THE INDUSTRY SEEN BY THE PUBLIC?

Land-based jobs aren't in the public eye as much as other industries. People are still learning about the different ways the sector affects our lives, for example, through landscape management, farming and environmental management. The growing interest in caring for the environment is helping to increase public understanding of what rural life is about today.

Some areas of work such as sports turf management and landscape design are becoming much more popular and there is growing interest in careers in forestry and conservation.

The secret of career satisfaction is to find the job that suits you – your interests, skills and personality. It's best to focus on doing your research into what job is right for you instead of planning your career around what other people think.

HOW EASY IS IT TO GET PROMOTED?

There are plenty of opportunities for energetic, hard-working individuals to get on. But it's important to be aware that there are better prospects in some job areas than in others. For example, larger organisations will have the scope to allow employees to move up the career ladder, whilst in smaller organisations this is not possible. In some areas of the industry, promotion often means changing jobs or even location.

> ### DID YOU KNOW?
>
> In the UK we consume a huge amount of timber, paper, boards and sundry wood products each year — equivalent to around 50 million cubic metres — that's around two large trees per person!

WHAT ABOUT WORKING ABROAD?

There are some good opportunities to work abroad. UK qualifications are well respected across the world, and the more highly qualified a person is, the better the chances of finding work. One important thing to remember is that the vast majority of the world does not speak English so anyone who is serious about working abroad needs to develop their language skills.

WHAT IF I WANT TO BECOME SELF-EMPLOYED?

This is much easier in some areas than in others. There are good opportunities for mechanics specialising in agricultural machinery and for landscape gardeners to set up their own business. The fact that the land-based industry is made up of so many small companies says a lot about the number of opportunities for self-employment. However, in some sectors the amount of money needed to set up in business is beyond the reach of most people. For example, farm managers wanting to become farm owners need to buy or lease large areas of land, which is so expensive it is not an option for many.

Anyone thinking about self-employment needs to develop their business skills. There's so much more to running a business than having a talent for a certain job. Designing beautiful gardens is great but making a living involves managing finances, labour, materials and dealing with customers. There's also the vital matter of promoting your skills to earn you enough money. It's a challenging but rewarding route and there is support out there. A good place to start could be your local Business Link.

See Chapter 13 for further information. You can find more on self-employment in *Working for Yourself Uncovered* by Andi Robertson, published by Trotman (www.trotman.co.uk).

11

PHIL HARWOOD

Case study 5

DRIVER-GARDENER, BIRMINGHAM CITY COUNCIL

Phil Harwood has worked in grounds and garden maintenance for Birmingham City Council for 26 years. He is currently employed by a contractor to the council. Phil is setting a bit of a family tradition as his father used to work as a council gardener and his son is now about to complete his third summer in the job!

I really enjoy the variety of my work. It's also very satisfying to bring green city spaces to life.

What activities does your job involve?

'I work as part of a group of driver-gardeners maintaining the green areas in Birmingham city centre's parks, streets and schools. We have a set "round" that we go through every fortnight. It includes schools, churchyards, parks, streets and old people's homes.

'We do some tasks every day such as tidying park areas up, emptying bins and checking the state of the playground equipment. Other jobs will be done when they're needed like repairing damaged trees. Then there are the seasonal tasks such as restocking the flower beds with plants and cutting the grass and hedges.'

What equipment do you use in your job?

'We work in what is known as a "triple" – one of us operates a ride-on mower with two of us following with grass strimmers. We also work with a range of gardening equipment such as hedge cutters, rotivators and mowers. We are fully trained up before we can use any equipment and also go on regular refresher courses to keep our practical skills up to date.

'Using specialist equipment and working outside in an urban area means that health and safety is a big part of my job. I'm always aware of what I'm doing and how it might affect members of the public, for example, making sure I don't leave grass cuttings on paths as this could cause people to slip. I also take good care of my own safety by wearing protective clothing and using equipment carefully.'

Do you work as part of a team?

'Because of the practical and large-scale nature of the work it's very rare that you work on your own in this job. I'm part of a three-man team.'

What are the main challenges and rewards of your job?

'Emptying park bins and dealing with dog mess are definitely the least pleasant parts of my job.

'Aside from those aspects I really like getting to work outside. It's especially good when it's sunny, but even in winter being out and about is still a great part of my job! I really enjoy the variety of my work. It's also very satisfying to bring green city spaces to life, for example, by planting new trees in a park.'

To find out more turn to Chapter 3, 'What are the jobs?' and Chapter 6, 'Training'.

12

The last word

Now you know about the many opportunities available in land-based industries – but is it the right sector for you?

After learning more about working outdoors and hearing from people in the sector, you should have a better idea of whether it is for you. There are good job opportunities for the right people and a great deal of job satisfaction, too. You are the best judge of whether you are suited to this type of work, and at this stage you may still not be sure. This is fine because this book is a starting point, giving an overview of the industry and the training opportunities within it. In such a varied industry, it's important to find out more before committing yourself to a particular career.

For anyone seriously interested in one of the careers mentioned in this book, a wise step would be to get some work experience. There's nothing like some hands-on experience and seeing for yourself exactly what a job is like. It may sound good on paper, but what about the realities of the job? You may have noticed that some of the people profiled in this book suggest volunteering or work experience as a valuable way to gain real insight into a job area. The long-term benefits of gaining personal experience of the job you're interested in should far outweigh the inconvenience.

Once you've gained some practical experience of a job and are sure that it's right for you, the next step is to look at how to get into it.

Could you move into your chosen job area with your current skills and qualifications? If not, what further training would you need?

Are you able to take up a full-time training course, or would you prefer to study part-time and earn some money at the same time?

What about the option to do a job with training that leads to a vocational qualification?

It's very likely you'll want to find out more about this varied and developing industry. Whatever your questions, there is help at hand. In the next section, you'll find details of organisations that can help you move forward towards an interesting and fulfilling career working outdoors.

If you have made it this far through the book then you should know if working outdoors is really for you. But, before getting in touch with the professional bodies listed in the next chapter, here's a final, fun checklist to show if you have chosen wisely.

QUIZ

✔ TICK YES OR NO

DO YOU ENJOY WORKING OUTSIDE?

☐ YES
☐ NO

DO YOU LIKE UNDERTAKING PRACTICAL, 'HANDS ON' TASKS?

☐ YES
☐ NO

ARE YOU SELF-MOTIVATED AND COMFORTABLE MANAGING YOUR OWN WORKLOAD?

☐ YES
☐ NO

DO YOU WANT A JOB WHERE YOU BALANCE A VARIED WORKLOAD WITH A REGULAR ROUTINE OF ACTIVITIES?

☐ YES
☐ NO

ARE YOU ABLE TO COMMUNICATE EFFECTIVELY WITH LOTS OF DIFFERENT PEOPLE?

☐ YES
☐ NO

ARE YOU A TEAM PLAYER?

☐ YES
☐ NO

If you answered 'YES' to all these questions then
CONGRATULATIONS! YOU'VE CHOSEN THE CAREER THAT SUITS YOU!
If you answered 'NO' to any of these questions then this may not be the career for you. However, there are still a range of options open to you, for example you could work as a sales person at a garden centre or farm shop or in an administrative role within an agricultural, environmental or other land-based organisation.

13

Further information

Listed in this section are contact details for organisations that can give you further information about education and training opportunities and job openings in land-based industries.

GENERAL INFORMATION

Connexions
Website: www.connexions.gov.uk
Careers information for young people, with links to local Connexions offices.

Edexcel
One90 High Holborn
London
WC1V 7BH
Tel: 01204 770696
Website: www.edexcel.org.uk
Information on a wide range of qualifications including BTECs, GCSEs and NVQs.

Lifelong Learning
Website: www.lifelonglearning.co.uk
Information on Career Development Loans – deferred repayment bank loans to pay for vocational learning or education.

Learning and Skills Council
Cheylesmore House
Quinton Road
Coventry
CV1 2WT
Tel: 0845 019 4170
Website: www.lsc.gov.uk
The Learning and Skills Council (LSC) is responsible for funding and planning education and training for over 16 year olds in England. The website contains details of training opportunities for both youth and adult learners.

In Scotland this work is undertaken by
Scottish Further and Higher Education Funding Council (SFC)
Donaldson House
97 Haymarket Terrace
Edinburgh
EH12 5HD
Tel: 0131 313 6500
Website: www.sfc.ac.uk

In Wales by
Education and Learning Wales
Tel: 0845 608 8066
Website: www.elwa.ac.org.uk

In Northern Ireland by
The Department of Education
Tel: 028 9127 9279
Website: www.deni.gov.uk

New Deal
Website: www.newdeal.gov.uk
(Part of the Department for Work and Pensions)
Website contains information for people claiming benefits on
the help and support available to help them look for work,
including training and job preparation.

UCAS
Website: www.ucas.ac.uk
Information on degree courses in the UK.

INFORMATION ON TRAINING AND JOB OPPORTUNITIES IN THE LAND-BASED SECTOR

Lantra
Lantra House
Stoneleigh Park
Nr Coventry
CV8 2LG
Tel: 0845 707 8007
Website: www.lantra.co.uk
Lantra is the Sector Skills Council for the land-based sector.
Its website contains a wide range of information on training
and careers with useful links to other websites.

Lantra Wales
Royal Welsh Showground
Llanelwedd
Builth Wells
LD2 3WY
Tel: 01982 552646
Website: www.lantra.co.uk/wales

Lantra Scotland
Newlands
Scone
Perth
PH2 6NL
Tel: 01738 553311
Website: www.lantra.co.uk/scotland

Napaeo
The Association for Land Based Colleges
Website: www.napaeo.org.uk
Napaeo is the Association of Further and Higher Education
Colleges which has specialist provision in land-based and
related subjects. Member colleges deliver full-time, part-time
and most forms of flexible learning courses, ranging from
pre-entry to postgraduate levels across most of the subject
areas. Courses include:

- Agriculture
- Animal Care
- Aquaculture
- Business Management
- Countryside Management
- Environmental Conservation
- Equine Studies
- Floristry
- Food Processing
- Game Conservation
- Horticulture
- Sport and Leisure
- Trees and Timber
- Veterinary Nursing.

Become instantly more attractive

INFORMATION ON SPECIFIC JOB AREAS

Agriculture

National Farmers' Union
Agriculture House
Stoneleigh Park
Stoneleigh
CV8 2TZ
Tel: 024 7685 8500
Website: www.nfuonline.com
Information on farming and links to major agricultural
colleges.

Farmers' Union of Wales
Llys Amaeth
Plas Gogerddan
Aberystwyth
SY23 3BT
Tel: 01970 820820
Website: www.fuw.org.uk

NFU Scotland
Head Office
Rural Centre-West Mains
Ingliston
EH28 8LT
Tel: 0131 472 4000
Website: www.nfus.org.uk

Environmental Conservation

Natural England (previously known as the
Countryside Agency)
1 East Parade
Sheffield
S1 2ET
Tel: 0114 241 8920
Website: www.naturalengland.org.uk

Countryside Council for Wales
Maes-y-Ffynnon
Penrhosgarnedd
Bangor
LL57 2DW
Tel: 0845 130 6229
Website: www.ccw.gov.uk

Scottish National Heritage
Great Glen House
Leachkin Road
Inverness
IV3 8NW
Tel: 01463 725000
Website: www.snh.org.uk

Rural Development Council Northern Ireland
17 Loy Street
Cookstown
Co Tyrone
Northern Ireland
BT80 8PZ
Tel: 028 8676 6980
Website: www.rdc.org.uk

Fencing

Fencing Contractors Association
Warren Road
Trellech
NP25 4PQ
Tel: 07000 560722
Website: www.fencingcontractors.org
The FCA is the fencing industry's trade association for the
fencing industry and is involved in legislation, standards and
training.

Fisheries

Institute of Fisheries Management
22 Rushworth Avenue
West Bridgford
Nottingham
NG2 7LF
Tel: 0115 982 2317
Website: www.ifm.org.uk

Forestry

Forestry Commission (England)
National Office
Great Eastern House
Tenison Road
Cambridge
CB1 2DU
Tel: 01223 314546
Website: www.forestry.gov.uk
The Forestry Commission is the government department
responsible for the protection and development of Great
Britain's forests. The website includes job opportunities.

Forestry Commission (Wales)
Victoria House
Victoria Terrace
Aberystwyth
SY23 2DQ
Tel: 0845 604 0845

Forestry Commission (Scotland)
Silvan House
231 Corstorphine Road
Edinburgh
EH12 7AT
Tel: 0131 334 0303

Forest Service (Northern Ireland)
(An agency within the Department of Agriculture and Rural
Development)
Forest Service
Dundonald House
Upper Newtonards Road
Belfast
BT4 3SB
Tel: 028 9052 4480
Website: www.forestserviceni.gov.uk

The Arboricultural Association
Ampfield House
Ampfield
Romsey
SO51 9PA
Tel: 01794 368717
Website: www.trees.org.uk
Website includes details of education and training
opportunities and job vacancies.

Institute of Chartered Foresters
59 George Street
Edinburgh
EH2 2JG
Phone: 0131 240 1425
Website: www.charteredforesters.org
Information and support for careers in forestry and
arboriculture.

Game and Wildlife Management

National Gamekeepers' Organisation Charitable Trust
PO Box 3360
Stourbridge
DY7 5YG
Tel: 01384 877748
Website: www.gamekeeperstrust.org.uk
Website includes careers advice and information on college
courses.

National Gamekeepers' Organisation
PO Box 107
Bishop Auckland
DL14 9YW
Tel: 01388 665899
Website: www.nationalgamekeepers.org.uk
Information on gamekeeping on the website, plus sections of
National Gamekeepers magazine online.

Horticulture

Royal Horticultural Society
80 Vincent Square
London
SW1P 2PE
Tel: 0845 260 5000
Website: www.rhs.org.uk
Website information on training, exams and horticultural
careers.

Land-Based Engineering

Institution of Agricultural Engineers
Barton Road
Silsoe
Bedford
MK45 4FH
Tel: 01525 861096
Website: www.iagre.org
The Institution of Agricultural Engineers (IAgrE) is the
professional body for engineers, scientists, technologists
and managers in agricultural and land-based industries.
The website includes information on qualifications and job
vacancies.

Landscaping

British Association of Landscape Industries
Landscape House
Stoneleigh Park
National Agricultural Centre
CV8 2LG
Tel: 0870 770 4971
Website: www.bali.org.uk
Website information on training and job vacancies.

The Greenkeepers' Training Committee
Aldwark Manor
Aldwark, Alne
York
YO61 1UF
Tel: 01347 838640
Website: www.the-gtc.co.uk
Website information on golf course greens, plus useful
training links.

INFORMATION ON VOLUNTEERING

Volunteering England
Regents Wharf
8 All Saints Street
London
N1 9RL
Tel: 0845 305 6979
Website: www.volunteering.org.uk
Information on volunteering opportunities and local volunteer
centres throughout England.

In Scotland this work is undertaken by
Volunteer Development Scotland
Stirling Enterprise Park
Stirling
FK7 7RP
Tel: 01786 479593
Website: www.vds.org.uk

In Wales by
Volunteering Wales
Website: www.volunteering-wales.net/

In Northern Ireland by
Volunteer Development Agency
129 Ormeau Road
Belfast
BT7 1SH
Tel: 028 9023 6100
Website: www.volunteering-ni.org/

British Trust for Conservation Volunteers
Sedum House
Mallard Way
Doncaster
DN4 8DB
Tel: 01302 388 883
Website: www.btcv.org.uk
Opportunities for environmental conservation placements, sessions and holidays.

Earthwatch Institute
Mayfield House
256 Banbury Road
Oxford
OX2 7DE
Tel: 01865 318 838
Website: www.earthwatch.org/europe
An international environmental charity which matches volunteers with overseas conservation projects.

The National Trust
Community, Learning and Volunteering
Heelis
Kemble Drive
Swindon
SN2 2NA
Tel: 01793 817400
Website: www.nationaltrust.org.uk
Full-time and one-off volunteering placements.

Voluntary Service Overseas
Head office
317 Putney Bridge Road
London
SW15 2PN
Tel: 020 8780 7200
Website: www.vso.org.uk
International development charity which organises overseas
work placements for volunteers.

The Wildlife Trusts
The Kiln Waterside
Mather Road
Newark
NG24 1WT
Tel: 01636 677711
Website: www.wildlifetrusts.org/
The largest voluntary organisation working in the UK on all
aspects of nature conservation with local Trusts.

INFORMATION ON THE SECTOR AND THE JOBS
www.afuturein.com
Lantra's career website for adults and young people
with information on the industry, the careers and work
experience.

www.land-force.org.uk
Land-based vacancies

The *Guardian* newspaper
Environmental jobs section every Wednesday

Local government jobs
www.lgjobs.com

Forestry Commission vacancies
www.forestry.gov.uk

Agriculture magazines
Farmers Weekly
Farming News
Farming Life
The Scottish Farmer

Fish Farming magazines
Fish Farmer
Fish Farming International

Horticulture magazine
Horticulture Week

INFORMATION ON SELF-EMPLOYMENT

Business Eye in Wales
www.businesseye.org.uk

Business Gateway Scotland
www.bgateway.com

Business Link
www.businesslink.gov.uk

Invest Northern Ireland
www.investni.com

USEFUL BOOKS
Careers 2008, Trotman
Working in Agriculture and Horticulture, Connexions
Working with Animals, Connexions
Working with Animals, Victoria Pybus, Vacation Work
Working with the Environment, Tim Ryder and Deborah
Penrith, Vacation Work